Six-word Lessons on

Female Asperger
Syndrome

100 Lessons to Understand
and Support Girls and
Women with Asperger's

Tracey Cohen

Published by Pacelli Publishing
Bellevue, Washington

Six-Word Lessons on Female Asperger Syndrome

Published by Pacelli Publishing
9905 Lake Washington Blvd. NE, #D-103
Bellevue, Washington 98004
Pacellipublishing.com

ISBN-10: 1-933750-45-6
ISBN-13: 978-1-933750-45-3

Introduction

I always knew I was different.

As did my loving mother from the time I was an infant.

But we did not understand why, and unfortunately knowledge of Asperger syndrome, especially relevant to girls, was scarce.

Short enough to be read in a day, recommended resources for anyone compelled to learn more, it is my sincere intention that this book serve as a concise, powerful, valuable tool for individuals, families, educators and medical professionals.

I am forever grateful to each and every friend, acquaintance and family member who has shown me kindness, tolerance and understanding over the years.

Peace, love and happiness to all.

~ Tracey Cohen

Foreword

I first met Tracey and her mother at her evaluation to determine if she had a diagnosis on the autism spectrum. Tracey is an intelligent young woman and I am so glad she is sharing her story so that her experiences can help others in similar situations.

This is a powerful and emotional book written from the first-hand experience of a gifted and talented young woman with Asperger's. She shares her life-long battle to discover her true self and find answers to the questions she always wondered about. The book shares her incredible story from her childhood through today.

Tracey has put her heart and soul into this book, and I believe it shows. Her lessons will resonate with many who read it and will transform lives.

This book is such a valued resource, not only for girls and women who are on the autism spectrum, or believe they might be, but also for those who love and care for them. From teachers, professionals, and parents, to the individuals who are seeking out an Autism Spectrum diagnosis for themselves, this book will provide a unique and powerful insight into what the journey and struggles have been for Tracey and her family, providing an understanding that I don't believe can be found anywhere else.

Asperger's Syndrome wasn't officially recognized as a diagnosis until the mid-1990s, over fifty years after autism was identified. Dr. Hans Asperger identified the diagnosis based on behavioral observations of four boys. Even to this day, there is little research on the differences in male and female symptoms, which makes this book so valuable.

For many years, many girls and women have often gone unidentified and misdiagnosed. Males and females share the same diagnostic behaviors, but girls and women present these symptoms to the world and cope with them extremely differently from their male counterparts. Tracey explains these differences in her book.

Tracey has a unique way of not only telling her own story, but also explaining Asperger's syndrome and the challenges she faced, as well as the strength her diagnosis has given her throughout her life.

Her experiences, abilities and perspective on life growing up as an undiagnosed female with Asperger's will be appreciated by many who have been in her shoes, or may currently be in her shoes. Her story will also provide a greater understanding to those who work with, love and cherish these girls.

I believe this book is an essential part of providing a better understanding of females on the autism spectrum and is one that everyone should read.

Karen McKibbin
Portland Autism Center, Portland Oregon
March 2015

Acknowledgements

I would like to extend my sincere gratitude to all the noted professionals and leaders in the field of Asperger syndrome and autism spectrum disorder. Your work has provided me with invaluable insight resulting in a happier, healthier me.

I aspire to do the same for others in this book which I dedicate with much love to my parents, George and Joan Cohen, my staunch supporters, each in their own uniquely loving way.

Terminology

Asperger syndrome - an autism spectrum disorder largely distinguished by significant difficulties in social interaction and nonverbal communication. A neurological disorder, the exact cause of Asperger's is not known but believed to be genetically linked.

Aspie - a person who has Asperger syndrome

Neurotypical - a term originating in the autistic community to describe those who are not on the autistic spectrum.

Figures of Speech - I chose to use figures of speech (communication that is not meant literally) throughout the book in an attempt to implement humor, flow of content and appeal to the likings of neurotypical readers. The content itself however is not exaggerated in the least. To my aspie readers I apologize for any confusion and acknowledge that it takes years of practice to recognize and understand the euphemisms of the neurotypical world. For clarification, please reference TheFreeDictionary.com and/or contact me directly at **runtrace@hotmail.com**.

Contents

Detecting Early Signs of Asperger Syndrome...........................11

Why Are Females Missed in Diagnosis?.....................25

Seeking Diagnosis as an Adult Woman.....................35

Inside the Soul of an Aspie.........................47

Social Skills, a Complex Learning Process...........57

Navigating the Social World Aspie-Style...........69

Sensory Integration Difficulties: Over and Under..........79

Strategies for Coping with Sensory Challenges...........89

Change is Hard but Worth Embracing...................99

Tips Based on My Personal Experience........................111

Detecting Early Signs of Asperger Syndrome

1

Do not discount a parent's intuition.

A parent's sixth sense should never be ignored. Early on, my mother knew there was something not right with me, but professionals and family members trivialized her concerns. Unable to help me with early intervention, she has supported me through the years and played an integral role in my diagnosis process. Advocate for your child and trust your instincts unwaveringly.

2

Take notice of aversion to touch.

Though generally associated with classic autism, an infant's aversion to touch may be a red flag. As a newborn, instead of finding comfort in the closeness of being held, I would cry, become rigid and push away. Though I have tried many tactics, I still have trouble with intimacy, including the physical touch of another person.

3

Speech is advanced beyond their years.

The language of Asperger children tends to be more complex and formal than age would indicate. As a young child, I never babbled but spoke with purpose using minimal words to express a need or thought. Though I continually make efforts to refine my speech to be more socially appropriate, left to my natural tendencies and preferences, little has changed.

4

Smiles: gifts not givens for all

Signs of a child's ability to properly communicate with her environment can begin with a smile or lack thereof. As an infant, I rarely smiled. This natural reflex for most has eluded me throughout my life. A smile for me takes much work, and though I strive to achieve a joyful persona, near constant anxiety is my reality.

5

We are literal to a fault.

Aspies say what they mean and mean what they say. A 3:00 p.m. meeting does not mean 4:00 p.m. or even 3:15 p.m. We become agitated and confused when what we are told does not match reality. It has taken me a long time to realize that I must allow for these discrepancies in order to function in our neurotypical dominated world.

6

Even small changes can be devastating.

Aspies thrive on routine and do not tolerate even the smallest of changes. As a very young child, my parents, determined to replace the old stained carpet in my bedroom, thought my fierce resistance was that of a defiant toddler. They did not realize that taking away my familiar carpet was stripping me of my security.

7

Our memory is second to none.

Don't say it if you don't mean it...'cause your 'li'l' aspie will not forget. Even as a kindergartner, when a teacher promised to have test results back by a certain date, I expected no less. If follow-through did not happen, I asked the teacher for my results every day until it happened.

8

Preoccupation with age defying subject matter

Early in life, aspies typically develop special mature interests, consuming their attention. These interests may change for some, while lasting a lifetime for others. I, oddly enough, expressed an awareness and aversion to excess body fat at the ripe old age of two. Still with me today, I continually learn to refine and optimize this deep-rooted importance.

9

I was kicked out of preschool.

Maybe not literally. But as a toddler, my distress and inability to thrive in social environments were so apparent that my teacher felt it best I be removed from the classroom. If my behavior was volatile like many boys in similar situations, a referral to a specialist would likely have been recommended. Instead, my quietly expressed anguish was chalked up to immaturity.

10

Anything less than perfection is unacceptable.

Girls, even more so than boys, set very high standards for themselves, critical of anything less than perfection. As a young child, I never purposely misbehaved. If ever asked about something troubling me, I would only express, "I want to be a good girl." This desire and need to be perfect has remained constant throughout my life.

11

Comfort trumps appearance; fashion be darned!

Aspies care more about dressing and grooming for comfort and practicality than appearance or keeping up with the latest trends, which are often not understood or deemed important. Soft, baggy clothes are common, generally due to sensory issues, as is the preference of wearing the same outfit day in and day out.

12

No two children are the same.

It is important to remember that just as no two children are exactly alike, no two children will duplicate the ways in which they display signs and symptoms of Asperger syndrome. Listen to your child and be open to recognizing atypical behavior as something they are trying to tell you rather than thinking they are being defiant.

Why Are Females Missed in Diagnosis?

13

Its namesake disregarded prevalence in girls.

Named after Austrian pediatrician Hans Asperger for his work in 1944, Hans primarily studied boys and originally did not believe there to be any existence of the condition in girls. More research is still needed to determine why and how Asperger syndrome affects genders differently.

14

Females are more expressive than males.

Even as children, girls are often better able to express themselves verbally than their male counterparts. In effect, girls are less likely to react aggressively when feeling upset and overwhelmed. Milder behavior draws less attention and urgency for follow-up on potential problems.

15

Girls' special interests appear age appropriate.

While the intensity and vast knowledge of girls' interests are no less than boys, they typically are more practical. Combined with the desire to please and fit in, red flags are less likely to be raised until girls fail to outgrow or elevate these interests to a more mature level.

16

Girls can be mighty fine actresses.

Females are generally better at role playing than males, and because we want to please and fit in, mimicking our peers, role models, or even television personalities is fairly common. I still observe those around me, always in search of that seemingly elusive wisdom which will help me to better navigate the neurotypical world.

17

Our competence makes achievements appear effortless.

Females, often more than males, are proficient at and care more about earning good grades, emulating socially acceptable behavior and receiving the approval of their peers. What is frequently overlooked is the effort it takes to achieve what is perceived to be normal. I still meltdown daily due to the overwhelming stress involved in getting through each day.

18

Girls sometimes help their aspie peers.

Generally less predatory and more nurturing than boys, aspie girls are less likely to be bullied by their female classmates and are sometimes even taken under the wing of a more socially adept counterpart. This allows girls with Asperger syndrome to further slide under the radar of having any real problem requiring professional help.

19

Wallflowers don't usually raise much concern.

Female aspies' tendencies to be subdued and eager to please combined with our ability and desire to fade into the woodwork, especially in social and group settings, camouflages off-putting behaviors. Lack of raucousness causes authority figures to leave well enough alone, attributing questionable behavior to immaturity and quirkiness.

20

Clinician inexperience with the female expression

Correct diagnosis of female aspies is dependent on the clinician's knowledge of characteristics specific to females. My first encounter proved frustrating and unsuccessful. Years later, armed with better knowledge and a referral by Dr. Tony Attwood, the kindness and expertise of Dr. Karen McKibbin provided the answers I had been seeking for a lifetime.

Seeking Diagnosis as an Adult Woman

21

With knowledge comes enlightenment and healing.

I was thirty years old when I learned about Asperger syndrome, and thirty-nine when I was officially diagnosed. This discovery has brought my family and me great insight into the hardships I incurred throughout my life, as well as the many misunderstandings between us. Knowing about Asperger's has allowed our relationship to strengthen and grow.

22

We're never too old to learn.

Having a name and documented reason for many of the difficulties I have and continue to face in life has opened up a world of resources, allowing me to continue to grow and find coping mechanisms for the seemingly simple things in life that non-aspies often take for granted.

23

Being unaware your leg is broken ...

...is an analogy I like to use to explain what it's like for aspies trying to navigate the neurotypical world without the innate tools privileged to most. We limp along in pain despite our best efforts, wondering how peers, family, strangers even, glide along effortlessly. Identifying a reason for shortcomings provides the means to make adjustments and help eliminate self-doubt.

24

Wrong treatment can cause more problems.

Incorrect diagnosis or none at all can lead to treatment of misleading conditions causing harm rather than healing. As a child, I was institutionalized for issues symptomatic of a bigger problem never addressed. "Treatment" taught destructive behaviors and thoughts that were carried into my adult years. Receiving my Asperger's diagnosis has been integral in allowing me to right many wrongs.

25

Correct diagnosis might take multiple attempts.

When I first sought diagnosis, I had learned about Asperger syndrome but not of the differences in therapists. Despite an initial unsatisfactory experience, I continued learning, and after speaking with noted expert Dr. Tony Attwood, sought a second opinion/diagnosis from Dr. Karen McKibbin, PsyD who specializes in adult women with Asperger's.

26

Family involvement is important for diagnosis.

Over the years, I learned strategies to function in the neurotypical world. An important part of my diagnosis involved interviews by the therapist to learn about my capabilities and tendencies, past and present, based on my memory and perception, as well as those who know me best. I was fortunate to have my mother's support in completing this process.

27

Find a professional familiar with women.

Diagnoses and therapists are not one-size-fits-all. Before seeking diagnosis, take time to research professionals who understand the differences between males and females and have the tools needed to diagnose adults versus children. Like medical doctors, therapists practice in various specialties.

28

How to find a qualified therapist

Read, ask questions and don't be shy about it. The Autism Society of America has local affiliates in nearly every state which include material specific to Asperger syndrome. Information through the online community can be found in mass, though I would encourage as much direct networking as possible. Conferences, support groups and libraries are also wonderful resources.

29

So now you know...what now?

There was a bit of a letdown after receiving my diagnosis. Nothing changed, no great insights were apparent. It did, however, allow me to understand why many of the things that come naturally to most are difficult and virtually painful for me. I continue to learn and try to be more patient with myself.

30

Who needs to know and why?

Sharing your diagnosis is a personal decision. I take each situation on an individual basis. If I feel it relevant and believe a person has the mindset to comprehend all I care to reveal, I will confide when I feel it is appropriate.

31

You're an aspie so own it.

Easier said than done, but really, we have much to be proud of. While I recognize and work daily on my faults and limitations, I take much pride in my genuine honest, loyal, caring nature and strict sense of right versus wrong. These are all common aspie traits, even if we are often misunderstood.

Inside the Soul of an Aspie

32

First impressions rarely reveal true character.

"What you see is what you get" with aspies, but be sure you understand what you are seeing before drawing conclusions. Truly kind-hearted, our compassionate, loyal, honest spirits are often hidden behind rough exteriors. Take the time to get to know our hearts; I suspect you'll be pleased with what you find.

33

Don't misconstrue a formal, flat approach.

It takes a great deal of energy and recall for aspies to speak and interact with inflection and an assumption of familiarity even among friends and kin. Fatigue, anxiety and the inability to read a person or situation affects communication and should not be received as aloof. Different perhaps from the norm, our natural approach is no less well-intentioned.

34

We are socially clumsy and unaware.

The effortless flow of conversation between non-aspie types baffles and amazes. While we struggle for words and clarification on when, what, how much information to share and inquire of others, neurotypicals seemingly take this all in stride. Our lacking does not indicate indifference but an innate skill for most that must be learned by people on the autistic spectrum.

35

Our focus supersedes common social graces.

Because they are so task-oriented, people with Asperger syndrome do not recognize that their drive to efficiently complete their work is perceived by others as aloof. Even on the job, social chitchat is the norm, prior to tackling the task at hand. While I am now more aware, I continue to struggle with this regularly.

36

Don't ask if truth isn't required.

When asked a question, we believe an honest answer is required, not placating another's ego. Keeping in mind our literal minds, it's important to understand we are not being unkind if, for example, we answer, "No, I don't like your haircut," as we are simply answering the question asked. It is not in our nature to speak untruths, because that is seen as counterproductive.

37

It is either right or wrong.

Aspies have a very strong sense of right versus wrong. It is incomprehensible to knowingly do something immoral, and we become enraged by others who engage in deceitful behavior. Excuses are not tolerated, and we are extremely hard on ourselves when we personally make mistakes, no matter how unintentional.

38

We are logical not purposefully defiant.

Aspies are practical, rational people. We are rule followers, not actively belligerent. But if we are asked to do something that does not make logical sense to us, we will balk, ask why and likely follow our own best judgment if not convinced otherwise. We aim to please but not at the expense of our personal code of conduct.

39

Change is devastating for an aspie.

Many people do not like change but for a person with Asperger syndrome, its effect goes much deeper than that. Even something as seemingly simple as new carpet in our home rocks our very core, adding another element of instability and distrust to the unpredictable world in which we live.

40

Comprehension isn't always indicative of performance.

Aspies can appear more competent than is accurate. Often lacking is our ability to plan and break down tasks into manageable progressions. Even when the work involved is understood, we may have no idea how to execute. Embarrassment and fear of failure and dismissal paralyzes our efforts along with the willingness to ask questions and admit deficiencies.

Social Skills, a Complex Learning Process

41

It's the hallmark of Asperger syndrome.

While no two aspies are the same, significant difficulty with social interaction and nonverbal communication is a common thread for all. Learning and progress can and will happen with diligent effort but is not a natural process as generally seen in neurotypicals.

42

The rules are endless and inconsistent.

Socializing is difficult, but the ever-changing precedents for appropriate behavior relevant to individual people and situations is nightmarish for aspies, especially considering neurotypicals do not always follow their own rules! When possible, seek counsel of a "real friend" willing to patiently explain perplexing situations and not embarrass you when "goofs" happen.

43

The white lie–a neurotypical conundrum

While common among non-aspies to exaggerate and be untruthful about trivial affairs, I do not value or promote this practice. I appreciate tact, and keeping negative, potentially hurtful opinions unspoken unless requested or necessary for a goal. I would not volunteer sentiment about a friend's unflattering attire, but if sought, would gently share my opinion.

44

The natural flow of daily conversation

This is not so natural for many aspies. An earnest if befuddled student, I study the exchanges of my neurotypical counterparts in my quest to learn the secret to their back and forth conversations akin to well-played tennis matches. Nevertheless, communications remain strained, words and innuendos lost on my literal mind, attention and endurance insufficient to persevere in unnecessary chatter.

45

Focus on timing, tact and tone.

Often it's not what is said but how and when. Aspies are not naturally cognizant of periphery factors including tone of voice, facial expressions, interrupting, and the practice of engaging in social graces before addressing our intent. As we learn to recognize opportune moments and control our timbre and outward appearance, more favorable results should prevail.

46

Practice helps, does not make perfect.

Socializing may not get easier for aspies, but avoidance makes it more difficult. Frequency allows for learning, motivation and friendships to thrive. Advance research of potential conversation topics, appropriate dress code, "exit strategy" if needed, proves helpful. Success enables pride; difficulties amount to differences and should not dissuade us from living life to our fullest potential.

47

We all need and want friends.

This includes people on the autism spectrum. Quirks, need for space, clumsy social graces notwithstanding, we long to be loved, needed, included, and appreciated by others. Our ideas and constraints of friendship might vary from the norm, but to have an aspie friend is to have a loyal, honest, dependable, caring person in life.

48

Avoid being possessive of your friends.

Aspies tend to have narrow focus, challenged by the "larger picture." As a child, I interacted with one friend at a time, distressed when that person wanted to socialize with others. Though I still struggle with these emotions, I realize the importance of having multiple, unique relationships, allowing others to do the same without offense or comparison.

49

Relationships are tough, aspie or not.

Platonic, romantic, aspie, neurotypical, no matter the form, relationships require work in order to thrive. Through a lifetime of learning, I now understand that if I wish to be accepted, quirks and all, I must extend the same to others. Doing so makes for a stronger, better me, enriching my life as well as those with whom I choose to surround myself.

50

Mistakes will happen; apologize, move forward.

Aspies strive to be perfect and attach the concept of permanence to most facets of life. Our emotional responses are immediate and intense; we fear social snafus jeopardize any redemption. But neurotypicals generally overcome their reactions quickly. Good can result if we apologize and learn from our mistakes.

51

Never say never; anything is possible.

Years ago when I began running races, being in the mere presence of others was a feat. A successful conversation, even a simple hello came next. Recognition followed, and now the running community embraces me. I am still awkward, if less so, and easily overwhelmed but grateful for the acceptance and kindness bestowed which I never thought possible.

Navigating the Social World Aspie-Style

52

Aspies don't possess inherent social skills.

People with Asperger syndrome lack the inherent ability to understand, recognize and process many of the social skills that come naturally to most. Eye contact is difficult at best. Non-verbal cues, innuendo, sarcasm, pranks–much of this is lost on our literal minds, which leads to misunderstandings, awkward situations, embarrassment and anxiety.

53

Aspies' definition of what constitutes social

The store, work, a joint home, and an outing with friends all embody social elements. While our social appetites vary, situations involving one or more people constitute a puzzle to be evaluated and solved. Refuge from our world's social vortex is sought and found where there are no people, no social rules to comprehend and follow; only quiet, peaceful solitude.

54

Having "fun" can require maximum effort.

Conventional social gatherings for aspies may entail more work than play. We struggle to know what to say and how to act. Without a role we are lost. Functions like volunteer work, which provide a specific purpose, may work best as social entertainment. With a goal in mind and partial script to follow, interacting with others is not quite as daunting.

55

Tolerance for social interaction is low.

There is a concept often referred to as a "social bucket." People with Asperger syndrome are equipped with merely a cup. Some days our cup is slow to fill while others find it overflowing before the day is yet to begin, making even the best-intentioned social interactions exhausting and overwhelming.

56

Common processing delays in social settings

People with Asperger syndrome can become quickly overwhelmed in social situations, often resulting in a delay of processing. What may appear to be disregard for instructions given or information shared, is more likely a lack of understanding or an inability to express interest in the topic at hand.

57

We get overexcited sharing our passions.

Females especially are often able to hide social awkwardness under the guise of being shy–except when speaking of our all-consuming passions, generally more conventional than our male counterparts. Slow to notice disengagement of our audience, we are labeled self-centered when candor would be appreciated to help us understand and fix our shortcomings.

58

Where have I heard that before?

Aspies will memorize favorite movie and television scripts, emulating mannerisms of those we admire. I come armed to social situations with one-liners and topics of conversation in an attempt to maintain fluid conversation. Unfortunately, awkward silence usually ensues after I have used up my scripted material, only to think of things to say long after the opportunity has passed.

59

Don't be fooled by facial expressions.

Or lack thereof. Aspies lack the natural ability to display emotion. This absence is often reflected in our face, making it appear lackluster. This does not mean feelings are not percolating inside, but our emotional response is often delayed, and while it can be taught, we struggle to understand how to express ourselves, both verbally and nonverbally.

60

Please don't tell us to relax.

For people with Asperger syndrome, there is much stress and anxiety involved in handling even the basics of daily living, much requiring social interaction which we work very hard to execute correctly. Those who accept and celebrate our quirks as opposed to trying to change who we are will help us to feel more at ease.

Sensory Integration Difficulties: Over and Under

61

Aspies experience hyper and hypo senses.

Sensory sensitivities are common among people with Asperger syndrome. We may experience any one of our seven senses intensely or virtually not at all, often resulting in anxiety and physical pain. Also challenging is their unpredictability from week to week, sometimes even day to day, further complicating treatment and coping mechanisms.

62

Loud to you, painful for me

As a child, I was scolded for becoming agitated when my environment was too loud. Its effect, equivalent to repeatedly banging my head with a hammer, was not recognized. I can clearly hear conversations from afar and am unable to block out background noise. Challenged in this way my entire life, some aspies face the opposite problem.

63

Touch–another complicated mode of communication

Many aspies, including myself, find touch difficult at best, painful in many instances. We rebuff physical contact and affection, seemingly an indication that we do not wish to be bothered, when our reality is an inherent need of space. We default to this innate mode of self preservation in our attempt to avoid sensory overload.

64

The subjective eye of the beholder

Visual processing is a challenge for many on the autism spectrum. Clumsiness due to poor depth perception, blurred, distorted vision and hypersensitivity to lighting are common problems. I personally struggle with brilliant, artificial lights which make my head feel as though it will explode, as does focusing on whole objects versus specific details.

65

Aspies taste everything or virtually nothing.

Aspies affected by a hyposensitive palate tend to have a penchant for very spicy foods and may even seek to chew on non-edible items such as pebbles and clay to satisfy their cravings. Inversely, those experiencing hypersensitive taste buds may choose to rigorously restrict their diet to avoid the discomfort associated with overstimulation.

66

Odors may be over or underwhelming.

Some aspies have no sense of smell, but I am challenged by the opposite extreme. Once, woken by a housemate opening the refrigerator in the next room, I detected the seemingly unmistakable odor of alcohol. I learned the following day there was no alcohol in the house. The scent I detected was fermenting grapes at the back of the cooler.

67

There are reasons for our movements.

Many aspies experience difficulties with their vestibular system. Some appear klutzy, while others, who are hyposensitive, tend to exhibit peculiar displays of movement to satisfy sensory needs. When I was a teenager, I kicked my leg at random. Though humiliated by the mockery of my peers, it took some time for me to find a more suitable outlet.

68

Body awareness is a complex phenomenon.

We invade your personal space; we bump, trip, maybe refuse to wear shoes with laces or clothing with buttons due to poor motor skills. Proprioception, or the awareness of the position of the body, is another area in which many aspies endure hypo or hypersensitive anomalies resulting in seemingly abnormal behaviors, along with increased stress and anxiety.

Strategies for Coping with Sensory Challenges

69

Identification is really the first step.

Understanding and acknowledging problems faced is vital to helping ourselves and those we love. As a child, I was not able to communicate my sensory difficulties. With experience, I began to recognize my "triggers" and learn to work around them. Aspie supporters should be aware that we do not act without reason. Learning the rationale behind behaviors is very important.

70

Sound: communicate, diminish or avoid it.

Visual aids can help people who are hyposensitive to sound; Earplugs, closed doors and music may help those who are hypersensitive. For myself, I find it most effective to request the offending noise be turned down when possible. Prior knowledge of the environment is especially helpful, allowing me to avoid when possible or at least eliminate the element of surprise.

71

Don't assume; ask before you touch.

It's best to ask before embracing an aspie. Touch for me is usually painful and uncomfortable rather than pleasant and comforting, regardless of my desire. When I am able to succumb to touch, heavy, deep pressure is needed as light touch makes me want to jump out of my skin. Communication better allows positive sensory and emotional experiences for aspies and neurotypicals alike.

72

Helping our visual needs and attributes

Sunglasses, dim lighting, and blackout curtains may help aspies whose sight is over-sensitive. Consistent visual supports may help under-sensitive vision. I find being aware of my surroundings and eliminating the element of surprise is half the battle. Though initially awkward, figuring out and communicating my needs when possible proves helpful even if accommodation is not always provided.

73

Customize diet for the body's preferences.

While my own hypersensitive palate, along with my willingness and ability to consume a variety of foods and textures continually evolves, undressed foods have always worked best. Over time, I have learned to tune into what my body craves. Hyposensitive appetites may enjoy spices on any number of foods, varying shapes, textures and consistencies.

74

Scented or not, we have options.

Aspies and their supporters have the luxury to choose between fragrant and unscented products. While uncontrolled environments prove more difficult, under-sensitive types must rely more on other senses. Those whose olfactory systems work on overdrive might find it necessary to avoid certain situations or respectfully request an offending odor be lessened, even eliminated.

75

Practice, practice, practice! Progress will happen.

Aspies with hypersensitive vestibular systems must not be deterred. While difficult, the more we work on our balance, the more skilled we will become and the better our chances of overcoming our related misgivings. Mastery is not a given, but with effort, improvement can happen. Athletics and activities such as yoga can help.

76

Navigating life's bumpy road with care

Many aspies have difficulty recognizing where their body exists relevant to other people and objects. Practicing the "arm's length rule" can help with personal space, and the use of a stylish walking stick may help with navigation. Those experiencing hyposensitive difficulties may benefit from practicing fine motor skills with any fun, simple activity such as "Play-Doh" or scrapbooking.

Change is Hard but Worth Embracing

77

It's constant in our unpredictable world.

Like it or not, change is inevitable. For this reason, no matter how unnatural, we would do ourselves justice to accept and prepare rather than fight against it. Challenging for sure, but I find it helpful to at least acknowledge it. Also, while not always successful, many times I try to invoke change before it happens to me.

78

Not even rules are above modification.

Aspies have a natural tendency to consider rules finite in nature. We, at least in part, allow rules to dictate behavior even when we unknowingly misinterpret their true meaning and intention. For this reason alone, the realization that rules can be tweaked and applied as relevant should be seen and practiced as a liberating development.

79

Sometimes the small changes are hardest.

As a child, I was devastated when my parents dared to replace the vomit-stained carpet in my bedroom. What is apparent to me now but I could not understand or verbalize then, is how important the smallest of details are in providing stability and comfort in our ever-changing world. It took time, but I eventually learned to appreciate the new, improved carpet.

80

Advance notice can help us cope.

Information given ahead of time allows aspies to prepare for and begin the process of adjustment to whatever inevitable shift is to come. Because my immediate reactions can be quite intense, I prefer written communication, allowing me to process in private and gain control over my emotions before interacting with others.

81

Having a backup plan is invaluable.

Avoidance of situations based on fear of the unpredictable leads to missed opportunities and stagnation. I find that having a backup plan to accommodate potential change allows me to take more risks with less anxiety, and while nothing is foolproof, this strategy helps me expand my horizons and cope with everyday living.

82

Sometimes it's actually a good thing.

Difficult days will happen, but as bad as things may seem, hard as it may be to remember, nothing lasts forever, and "change is inevitable." Furthermore, and perhaps more important: recognize what is not working and invoke change to make things better. Easier said than done, but important for quality of life.

83

Adventure makes routine all the sweeter.

I equate routine to a warm blanket on a cold day which can unknowingly become suffocating. Hence, I force myself to evaluate situations, stepping outside my routine when the pros outweigh the cons. No matter how extensive or minute the experience, once my goal is complete, that familiar blanket is waiting, providing warmth and security until my next exploit.

84

If at first you don't succeed...

Try, try again. When attempts at something new or even familiar fail, be mindful that this does not have to be indicative of the future and "change is inevitable." Take stock of what went well, modify areas that did not and remember true failure only really occurs when we do not use our experiences as opportunities to learn and improve.

85

I've always done it this way.

It is a harsh, cold reality when we are forced to abandon our norm and take on a new perspective. On the flipside, once entrenched in a new routine, sometimes I realize I was harboring false realities, and that my former beloved familiar routine was in actuality no longer entirely pleasant, relevant or beneficial to me.

86

Take one day at a time.

Finding the ability to squash counter-productive speculation, and focusing instead on the present allows for decreased anxiety and greater success, especially when confronted with impending change. Admittedly, I never thought this possible to achieve, but years of practice and discipline has yielded positive results.

Tips Based on My Personal Experience

87

"Good-natured" teasing has lasting effects.

I stem from a family that likes to express affection by harmless, friendly teasing. Sadly, my distress and literal internalization of the gibes was not recognized, leaving me feeling scorned. Though I now understand their intention, the resulting inept, insecure feelings that festered for so many years have proven difficult to rid myself of completely.

88

Careless words can endure a lifetime.

Similar to teasing, aspies comprehend words literally. I have never forgotten harsh words directed at me as a child and throughout my life. Neurotypicals are better equipped to dismiss thoughtless words and angry rants, but aspies internalize it, leading to years of hurt, broken relationships, and destroyed self-confidence. For me, time has dulled the pains though the scars remain.

89

Life isn't always fair or logical.

Though still often caught off guard when I cannot make sense of any number of situations, I try to remember that it does no good to pout; we can only control our own actions and reactions. As much as possible I do my best to take charge when appropriate and move on from situations of which I have no control.

90

Balance ambitious effort with necessary rest.

While I believe in stepping outside one's comfort zone, ample downtime is of equal importance. Without it, life becomes too overwhelming and works against our efforts. The right balance is a tricky, fickle variable relative to changing circumstances in our lives and the world at large, but it's best that we celebrate our achievements and regroup when we falter.

91

My favorite motto, "less is more"

Despite the fast-paced, demanding world in which we live, where bigger is deemed better by many, I find it helpful to focus on quality over quantity. Slow to process, easy to overwhelm, I am most successful when I focus on whom and what I believe important rather than trying to keep up with the norm.

92

Be willing to find middle ground.

While virtually unnatural for aspies to understand points of view other than our own, it is important to at least acknowledge those of others. Trying to force our will upon another is fruitless and is just as distasteful as when something is forced upon us. Learning to compromise or agreeing to disagree allows for a more harmonious state of being.

93

Disengage when in "full-fledged aspie mode."

Discussions will not be won, and tasks are best left incomplete when aspies are overwhelmed, brimming with anxiety, and in what I like to call "full-fledged aspie mode." An intense breed at our best, there is no reasoning with us when we are overwrought with emotion. Time alone to decompress is a must, even if we do not recognize the need ourselves.

94

Advice is optional, not an obligation.

No matter how well intentioned, never be coerced into following unwanted advice of others. Experience has taught my literal mind that what may work for the majority rarely benefits me. I have learned to express appreciation for suggestions, consider the options and follow my instincts as to what will best honor my personal needs and desires.

95

Aloofness is not akin to self-sufficiency.

Misplaced pride can get in the way of learning, making friends and general well-being. Negative experiences lead me to take on an "I don't need anybody, I can do it myself" kind of attitude, only to learn after years of hurt how counterintuitive such a derisive mindset really is.

96

Affection is not always inherently uncomplicated.

Be aware that an aspie's inability to appropriately give and receive affection is a neurological problem, not a choice or indication of indifference. On many occasions, I crave affection, but put in the position to give or receive, I often become agitated and stiff regardless of desire or intention.

97

Not wanting what other people want

As I find myself "wanting to want what most people want," I must remind myself that my unique aspie inspired needs and desires are just as valid as the next. And while my social threshold will never be that of neurotypicals, I must accept and stay true to myself, remaining thankful for all the blessings in my life.

98

Normal is a word, not reality.

Experience has taught me that "normal" is a concept which does not really exist. Humans--both aspies and neurotypicals-- are imperfect at best, each with unique idiosyncrasies, weaknesses, strengths, desires and goals. Learning to love and accept ourselves is essential for happiness, success and the respect we seek of our community at large.

99

Remember that others face challenges too.

No matter how difficult aspie challenges are, we must remember that neurotypicals face their own obstacles and demons. Different but likely no less daunting, it would behoove us all to check any and all self-pity at the door and alternatively, sympathize with, help and learn from our neighbors.

100

Above all, remember to be grateful.

Our challenges are many, but with them come numerous gifts. We must find our strengths and build on them. Remember that aspie or neurotypical, there is no perfection. Remaining appreciative for all that is good will lend itself to a more positive outlook and an openness, bringing added value into our lives.

References & Suggested Resources

Pretending to Be Normal – Living With Asperger's Syndrome, by Liane Holliday Willey, Aspie.com

The Complete Guide to Asperger's Syndrome, by Tony Attwood, TonyAttwood.com

Aspergirls, by Rudy Simone, help4aspergers.com

Autism Society, 4340 East-West Hwy, Suite 350, Bethesda, MD 20814, 800-328-8476, Autism-Society.org

National Autism Association, One Park Avenue, Suite 1, Portsmouth, RI 02871, 877.622.2884, NationalAutismAssociation.org

The Free Dictionary, By Farlex, Idioms.theFreeDictionary.com

GrowingUpAutistic.com, Books and resources for the autism community.

Contact Tracey

Encouragement, comfort, humor and insight are what I wish to provide. Please email me at **runtrace@hotmail.com** for speaking opportunities and any thoughts you care to share.

Let's connect on Facebook at **facebook.com/pages/Tracey-Cohen**

Thank you; I can't wait to "meet you."

About the *Six-Word Lessons Series*

Legend has it that Ernest Hemingway was challenged to write a story using only six words. He responded with the story, "For sale: baby shoes, never worn." The story tickles the imagination. Why were the shoes never worn? The answers are left up to the reader's imagination.

This style of writing has a number of aliases: postcard fiction, flash fiction, and micro fiction. Lonnie Pacelli was introduced to this concept in 2009 by a friend, and started thinking about how this extreme brevity could apply to today's communication culture of text messages, tweets and Facebook posts. He wrote the first book, *Six-Word Lessons for Project Managers*, then started helping other authors write and publish their own books in the series.

The books all have six-word chapters with six-word lesson titles, each followed by a one-page description. They can be written by entrepreneurs who want to promote their businesses, or anyone with a message to share.

See the entire *Six-Word Lessons Series* at 6wordlessons.com